D1308106

U.S. ★ WARPLANES
THE F-14 TOMCAT

ADRIAN GARDNER

the rosen publishing group's
rosen
central

Published in 2003 by The Rosen Publishing Group, Inc.
29 East 21st Street, New York, NY 10010

First Edition

Library of Congress Cataloging-in-Publication Data

Gardner, Adrian.
The F-14 Tomcat / Adrian Gardner.
    p. cm. — (U.S. warplanes)
Summary: An examination of the machinery, specifications, technology, and capabilities of the F-14 with discussion of the plane's early development, combat history, and likely future.
Includes bibliographical references and index.
ISBN 0-8239-3870-0 (library binding)
1. Tomcat (Jet fighter plane)—Juvenile literature. [1. Tomcat (Jet fighter plane) 2. Fighter planes.] I. Title. II. Series.
UG1242.F5 G36 2003
623.7'464—dc21

2002007901

Manufactured in the United States of America

CONTENTS

The story of the F-14, one of America's mightiest fighter planes, begins in the midst of the Cold War, a period spanning roughly forty-five years that began in the aftermath of World War II. This "war" gained its name because the era was marked by a strained, but largely peaceful, hostility between two global leaders—the United States of America and the Union of Soviet Socialist Republics (USSR). While the two nuclear superpowers never squared off against each other directly in a "hot" war, they did engage in an extremely expensive arms race and got involved in various "proxy" wars in which they funded or fought alongside communist and anticommunist forces of third countries. Each country was committed to being first among nations and establishing its political ideology—democracy or communism—as the worldwide norm.

Eastern Europe, once in the stranglehold of Leninist Communism, experienced a radical shift toward the end of the twentieth century, when many Communist governments lost power, and democracy began to take hold. In this photograph, construction workers in eastern Germany dismantle a statue of Vladimir Lenin in Berlin.

The final decade of the twentieth century witnessed a stunning transformation of the political map. In the face of popular protests and a worsening economy, the

While the U.S. military had responded to threats from the Soviet Union for years during the Cold War, today's threats to Western security come from different places. The attacks of September 11, 2001, on the United States, including the deliberate crashing of a passenger plane into the Pentagon in Arlington, Virginia (just outside Washington, D.C.), signaled the beginning of a new era and a new kind of warfare with new enemies. Now, former enemies like the United States and Russia are working together in many ways to combat terrorism.

Communist nations of Eastern Europe that ringed the Soviet Union fell one by one and began the long, difficult process of transforming themselves into more free and open societies. The Soviet Union itself at first tried to preserve its Communist system, while introducing limited political and economic freedoms. Eventually, however, it collapsed under the growing momentum of the Eastern Bloc's disintegration (the Eastern Bloc was made up of several Communist Eastern European nations that were under the sway of the Soviet Union). What eventually emerged was a smaller nation, Russia, surrounded by several newly independent former republics, such as Ukraine and Lithuania. As Russia struggled to regain its former military, economic, and political glory, the United States entered the twenty-first century as the only global superpower.

Now, unthinkable as it may have been to everyone at the time, the two countries have gradually drawn closer over the years and cooperate on several issues of mutual concern. Perhaps the greatest of these is terrorism, which both nations regard as today's principal threat to the Western way of life. On September 11, 2001, the world witnessed the horror of such a threat when the World Trade Center in New York City and the Pentagon outside of Washington, D.C., were attacked by terrorists belonging to an organization called Al Qaeda, who turned hijacked passenger planes into weapons of mass destruction.

The international response to these attacks brought about global cooperation on a scale never before seen. One of these international joint ventures was a military exercise dubbed Operation Enduring Freedom. Intended to root out the leaders of Al Qaeda and its training camps in Afghanistan, the military effort involved the troops of several countries and the approval of many more, including Russia, now considered by the United States to be an important ally in this new war.

It is ironic that one of the warplanes leading the way in this international fight against terrorism in far-off lands was originally designed and manufactured back in the Cold War era, when Americans and Russians thought of themselves as mortal enemies. When the first F-14 fighter aircraft was delivered by the Grumman Corporation at the end of 1970, it was expected to protect U.S. ships at sea from Soviet bombers and engage in dogfights over European skies with Soviet MiG-21s and other enemy fighter planes. No one could have imagined that the F-14, or any other American fighters, would have to patrol American airspace on the lookout for hijacked airliners piloted by suicidal terrorists bent on mass destruction. But this is how the world has changed in little more than thirty years, and the F-14 family of aircraft has had to change along with it.

The development of the F-14 came about because of the need to improve the aging American fighters in use in the early days of the Cold War. Some form of upgrade was required if the United States was to maintain its competitive edge over the Soviet Union.

As a result, the U.S. Navy and the U.S. Air Force teamed up to explore the possibility of developing a fighter plane that would, as far as possible, be appropriate for the needs of both forces. The Tactical Fighter Experimental (TFX) program was born in the early 1960s. The aerospace companies Grumman Corporation and General Dynamics won the right to design the TFX aircraft, which would be designated the F-111.

The Sea Pig

Through this project, the General Dynamics F-111A strike aircraft was developed for the air force. A development program for a similar aircraft suitable for use in the navy was called the F-111B. It was based on the General Dymanics design but handled by Grumman. These were to have been the first aircraft designed to have as much in common with each other as possible. This would allow the expenses of design, manufacturing, spare parts, and maintenance to be kept low.

This theory made a lot of sense economically. In practice, however, there were serious glitches. The single largest problem that aerospace designers and manufacturers had in converting the air force's land-based F-111A for use in the navy as the proposed F-111B was its weight. Since the F-111B would have to take off and land from an aircraft carrier (in essence, a floating runway), it needed to be able to accelerate and brake extremely quickly, as the

THE F-111A was an experimental land-based strike aircraft developed by the air force. Based on the same design, the navy developed the F-111B, which would have to take off and land from aircraft carriers. Though 5,000 pounds lighter than the F-111A, the F-111B was still far too heavy to be able to take off and land on short runways provided by carriers. Because of its great weight and slowness, the F-111B earned the nickname Sea Pig, and the project was quickly killed by Congress.

length of a carrier runway is fairly short. This meant the plane also had to be light; extra weight would only increase the length of runway needed for its takeoff and landing operations.

At around 90,000 pounds (40,823 kilograms) in weight, the F-111A was far too heavy an aircraft to take off from a carrier at sea. The navy requested that any redesigned aircraft should ideally have a weight of less than 50,000 pounds (22,680 kilograms). When Grumman presented the F-111B for trials, it weighed in at a startling 85,000 pounds (38,555 kilograms). That effectively meant that the F-111B could be used only on the navy's largest aircraft carriers. From the start, then, the navy's new fighter plane was already almost useless.

Test flights of the F-111B earned it the nickname Sea Pig because of its extreme weight, slow speed, and limited maneuverability. Worse

The Tomcat's "sweep-wing" design is one of the elements that makes it an effective fighter. These movable wings allow for greater speed and maneuverability. Despite setbacks, including crashes that resulted in pilot deaths, the U.S. Air Force took delivery of the first Tomcats by 1973.

still, several pilots were killed during unsuccessful test flights. Only seven F-111B's had been built by the time Congress officially stopped funding the project in 1968. Grumman went back to the drawing board, as did four other American companies that the navy invited to propose new fighter designs under the so-called Navy Fighter Experimental (VFX) program.

The VFX

The VFX was to be a fighter with a two-man crew and tandem seating (when one pilot sits behind another rather than side by side). The navy wanted it to feature two engines, an advanced weapons system with powerful radar, an arsenal of air-to-air missiles of various ranges (long, medium, and short), and a mounted gun for short-range dogfights. Most important, the navy wanted the VFX to be able to land on

WHAT'S IN A NAME?

The navy officer responsible for coordinating the development of the next generation of fighter aircraft with the Grumman Corporation was Admiral Tom Connolly. "Tom's Cat," as the model under review became known, formed the basis for the official name "Tomcat" some years later. From World War II onwards, Grumman used the "cat" suffix with its fighters, including the F-8F Bearcat, the F-7F Tigercat, the F-4F Wildcat, and the F-6F Hellcat.

a carrier with a full load of weapons. It could not afford another 85,000-pound blunder.

Of the bids submitted to the VFX program in 1968 by Grumman, Ling-Temco-Vought, McDonnell Douglas, General Dynamics, and North America Rockwell, four offered the distinctive feature of "sweep wings," which allow aircraft to fly faster and make sudden quick maneuvers that are not possible with fixed-wing aircraft.

Grumman won the VFX bid in January 14, 1969, by offering the 303 model aircraft. The company first began to look at this aircraft in 1966 when it was testing certain areas of the doomed F-111B. The 303 was designed to deliver air superiority, escort capabilities (flying with bombers and other fighters and providing them cover), and a sea-based interception ability (carrier-based fighters that can head off attacks by enemy fighters). It would also feature Sparrow radar homing missiles, Sidewinder infrared homing missiles, Phoenix long-range missiles, and a 20-mm rotary cannon.

After winning the navy's approval of the design, the 303 was redesignated the F-14, and Grumman was awarded a research, development, test, and evaluation contract on February 3, 1969.

The Test Flight

Completing the F-14's first test flight was important to Grumman because the contract between the company and the navy stated that

F-14A TOMCAT DIMENSIONS

Wingspan (unswept): 64 ft. 1 in. (19 m 4 cm)
Wingspan (swept back): 38 ft. 2 in. (11 m 47 cm)
Length: 62 ft. 8 in. (19 m 10 cm)
Height: 16 ft. (4 m 80 cm)
Weight (empty): 40,104 lbs. (18,191 kg)
Weight (max takeoff): 74,348 lbs. (33,724 kg)
Ceiling: over 50,000 ft. (5,240 m)
Speed (cruise): 576 mph (921.6 km/h)
Speed (max): 1,544 mph (2,470.4 km/h); Mach 2.33
Range: 1,730 nautical miles
Crew: 1 pilot, 1 radar intercept officer
Unit cost: $38 million in 1971

Grumman would have to pay a penalty ($5,000 for each day late) if no test flight was performed before the end of December 1970. In fact, Grumman was able to make two test flights before this deadline. The first occurred on December 21, 1970, piloted by chief test pilot Robert Smythe and project test pilot William Miller. It went off without a hitch. On December 30, the same aircraft that flew just nine days previously took off from Grumman's Calverton Airport on Long Island in New York for its second test flight. It suffered a failure in a hydraulic pump, leading to a total loss of the plane's controls. The two-man crew had no choice but to eject from the aircraft, leaving the plane to crash short of the Calverton runway. The pilots, thankfully, received only minor injuries.

Despite this setback, the navy and Grumman wanted to continue with the development of the F-14. The navy wanted Grumman to deliver the first fully tested fighter aircraft in 1973, meaning that the company had around three years to perfect the design and deliver a safe, highly functioning fighter. Many glitches remained to be worked out. On June 30, 1972, prototype aircraft #10 crashed into the Patuxent River in Maryland while practicing for an air show,

The aerodynamic F-14 has an honored place in U.S. military history and for decades has distinguished itself in operations in Libya, Iraq, the Balkans, and, most recently in Afghanistan. This early model F-14A is still used in test flights at NAS Patuxent River, Maryland.

becoming the second unit to be lost. This crash killed test pilot Bob Millar, who had survived the crash of the second test flight of the first F-14 in 1970. Almost a year later, on June 20, 1973, a third plane, aircraft #6, was lost while in flight near Point Mugu, California. This time, one of the plane's onboard missiles incorrectly angled upward on launch and ruptured a fuel tank, causing a fire and forcing the crew to eject.

By this time, however, the navy had already taken official delivery of the F14-A Tomcat, and its honored place in U.S. Navy history was established.

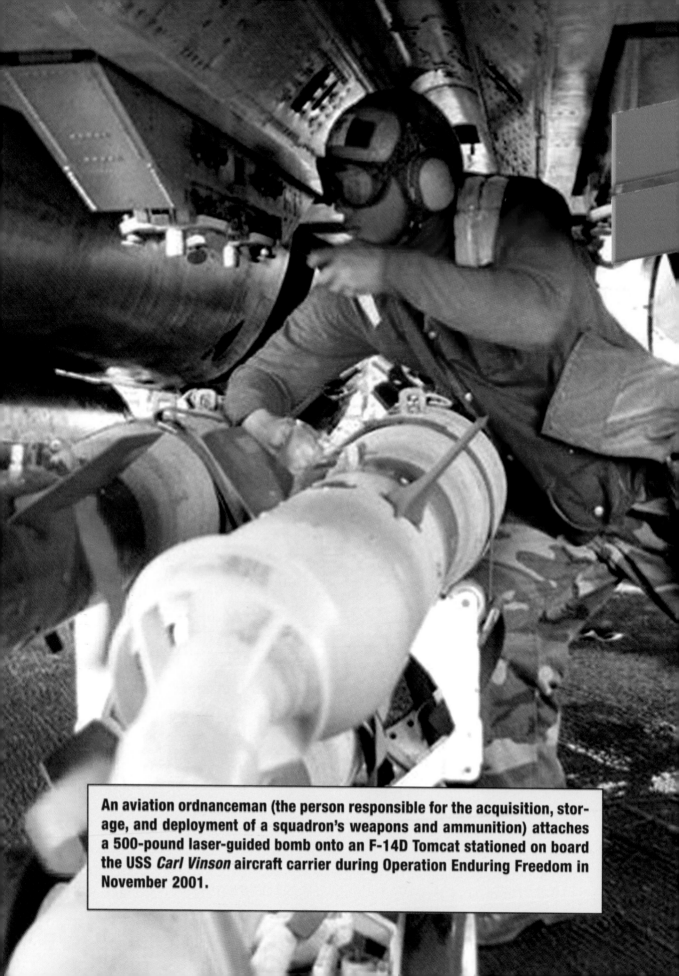

An aviation ordnanceman (the person responsible for the acquisition, storage, and deployment of a squadron's weapons and ammunition) attaches a 500-pound laser-guided bomb onto an F-14D Tomcat stationed on board the USS *Carl Vinson* aircraft carrier during Operation Enduring Freedom in November 2001.

2 THE TOMCAT'S CLAWS

While the F-14 is fully loaded with a variety of missiles and guns, weaponry is not its only strength. From top to bottom, wing to wing, the F-14 is designed for speed, maneuverability, and raw power.

Engines

When the first F-14 rolled off the production line, it was powered by two TF-30-P-412A turbofan engines designed by Pratt & Whitney. This engine was very similar to the one used on the canceled F-111B, and like that plane, it had its share of problems. The first was that the engines did not provide the F-14 with enough power. Early in the test flight programs, the engines would often stall when the plane was coming into or out of afterburner or when traveling at low speeds in high altitude.

The P-412A engine had another problem of a more catastrophic nature. From time to time, a fan blade would break off during flight, damaging the surrounding airframe structure and systems or completely destroying the engine and causing the loss of the aircraft. Yet it was only when an F-14's engine stalled when making a landing on the USS *John F. Kennedy*, forcing the plane to crash-land, that the navy and the Pentagon decided it was time to upgrade the engine to the P&W TF-30-P-414A in 1981. The P-414A did not entirely solve the stalling problem, nor did it possess any more thrust, but the steel cages around the first three fan blade compartments did offer some protection in the event of a fan blade failure.

With the engine performance being constantly assessed by the navy and its principal contractor, Grumman Corporation, it was expected that a more powerful engine would replace the P-414A. In July 1984, Grumman installed a pair of General Electric F101 engines

An F-14 takes to the skies during a test of its new General Electric F101DFE engines.

(later replaced by the F110-GE-400, an improved version of the F101 design) onto an F-14. The navy liked the improvement so much that it went ahead with its second aircraft construction program. Six test aircraft of the so-called F-14A+ were built, with the maiden flight made in September 1986. By November 1987, the F-14A+ was officially renamed the F-14B (of which thirty-eight new aircraft were built and thirty-two F-14As were upgraded to B status), and all of the P-412A engines in the F-14A models were replaced by the P-414A.

The more powerful GE engines allowed the F-14B to take off from an aircraft carrier without having to use its afterburners. This saved so much fuel that it gave the F-14B 60 percent more flying range and 33 percent more time in the air than the F-14A powered by the P-414A engines.

Weaponry

From its earliest conception, the Tomcat was designed to be equipped with the long-range air-to-air AIM-54 Phoenix missile, one of the primary weapons establishing the fighter's air superiority. With a range of up to 124 miles (200 kilometers), the Phoenix is the navy's only long-range air-to-air missile, and the F-14 is the only aircraft designed to carry it.

The missile was designed to work with the AWG-9 weapons control system, a radar developed by the Hughes Aircraft Company at its base in Culver City, California. The radar can track the positions of up to twenty-four airborne targets between 65 and 170 nautical miles away (depending on their size) and to altitudes of 100,000 feet (30,500 meters), while simultaneously selecting the six targets posing the greatest threat to the F-14. It can then launch the six loaded AIM-54 Phoenix missiles aboard the F-14 against those selected targets though most F-14s fly with only four Phoenix missiles because the impact of landing on carrier decks is too great with a load of six missiles. Because of the range of the Phoenix, all of this can be done without the F-14 even being seen by the enemy. Ironically, although it is such a powerful weapon, the Phoenix has never had occasion to be fired by American pilots in combat with enemy aircraft.

The Phoenix is fired by a solid-fuel rocket motor, which allows it to achieve a speed of between Mach 3.8 at low altitudes and Mach 5 at high altitudes and long distances (Mach 1 is the speed of sound; Mach 2 is twice the speed of sound.) Once launched, the Phoenix can be steered by three different types of guidance systems—autopilot, semi-active radar homing, and fully active radar homing. When fired at long-range targets, the missile usually begins on autopilot, following a preprogrammed course. Halfway to the target, a radar seeker mounted on the missile's nose takes over and responds to the F-14 radar signals bouncing off the target, adjusting its course if necessary. Once the missile draws to within 14 miles (22.4 kilometers) of the target, its own radar is activated to guide the missile for the final leg of the journey. This final stage of missile guidance is sometimes referred to as "fire and forget"; once the missile's radar takes over, the F-14 no longer needs to stay in the area to help guide the missile to its target.

The Sparrow

Other air-to-air missiles used by the F-14 include the AIM-7 Sparrow and the AIM-9 Sidewinder. The AIM-7M Sparrow entered service in 1983 and was the latest in a long line of Sparrows that began with

AIR-TO-AIR MISSILES USED BY THE F-14

AIM-54 Phoenix
    Contractor: Hughes Aircraft Company, Raytheon Company
    Powerplant (make): Solid-propellant rocket motor (Hercules)
    Length: 13 ft. (3.9 m)
    Diameter: 15 in. (38.1 cm)
    Wingspan: 3 ft. (90 cm)
    Weight: 1,024 lbs. (461 kg)
    Range: Over 100 nautical miles (over 184 km)
    Speed: Mach 4.3+
    Date deployed: 1974
    Unit cost: $477,000

AIM-7 Sparrow
    Contractor: Raytheon Company, General Dynamics Corporation
    Powerplant (make): Solid-propellant rocket motor (Hercules)
    Length: 12 ft. (3.64 m)
    Diameter: 8 in. (20 cm)
    Wingspan: 3 ft. 4 in. (1.02 m)
    Weight: 510 lbs. (231 kg)
    Range: 30 nautical miles (56 km)
    Speed: Mach 2.5
    Date deployed: 1976 (AIM-7F); 1982 (AIM-7M)
    Unit cost: $125,000–$165,000

AIM-9 Sidewinder
    Contractor: Raytheon Company, Loral and Ford Aerospace & Communications Corporation
    Powerplant (make): Solid-propellant rocket motor (Hercules)
    Length: 9 ft. 6 in. (2.98 m)
    Diameter: 5 in. (13 cm)
    Wingspan: 2 ft. 1 in. (63 cm)
    Weight: 190 lbs. (85.5 kg)
    Range: Over 9 nautical miles (over 16 km)
    Speed: Mach 2+
    Date deployed: 1956
    Unit cost: $41,000–$84,000

Navy personnel prepare a Phoenix missile for deployment on an F-14. Potentially one of the deadliest weapons in the navy's arsenal, it can be fired only by F-14s. However, it has never actually been fired by navy pilots in a combat situation.

the introduction of the AIM-7C in 1958. It is widely used by both U.S. and North Atlantic Treaty Organization (NATO) forces. It is a radar-guided missile that can be launched in all kinds of weather, at any altitude, and from any direction, day or night.

In its early days, the Sparrow did not enjoy a good reputation. It had been designed to attack large, slow objects, like bombers. When fired at quickly maneuvering or low-altitude targets, the Sparrow usually missed. During the Vietnam War, only 9 percent of Sparrows fired actually hit their targets.

However, more pilot training and technical enhancements gave the Sparrow a better success rate when used during Operation Desert Storm in 1991, when twenty-three Iraqi combat aircraft were shot down by AIM-7s (although most were fired from aircraft other than F-14s, such as the air force's F-15C Eagle). Changes to the missile's wing and an

Sparrows *(left)* and Sidewinders *(right)* are two of the missiles with which F-14 fighters are often equipped.

improved autopilot boosted its effectiveness. Its range was also doubled when it began to be launched by a more powerful dual-thrust booster/sustainer rocket. Improved electronics, such as an onboard computer, gave the missile greater success against small, speedy targets such as cruise missiles and low-flying antiship missiles.

The Tomcat usually carries two Sparrows. The missile is not a "fire and forget" weapon; the F-14 must continue to lock on its target with radar in order to guide the missile to a successful strike.

The Sidewinder

The Sidewinder, which first appeared in 1956, and has had numerous upgrades since then, is currently in service with the navy, the marines, and the air force. It is a heat-seeking, short-range missile whose guidance system homes in on the rear half of a target aircraft (where the heat of the plane's exhaust attracts the missile). Newer models can even detect the heat caused by the friction of air against a plane's wings, allowing the F-14 to fire a missile from anywhere in the sky, not just from behind its target. The infrared seeker allows the pilot to fire the missile at its target and then leave the combat area or take evasive action, since the Sidewinder will guide itself once it is launched.

The AIM-9M version, introduced in 1982, is the standard unit type and can better distinguish between enemy aircraft and decoy flares that are meant to draw a missile away from the actual target. Four Sidewinders can be loaded onto an F-14 (although it usually flies with only two) and can be used day and night, in all types of weather. The latest model sidewinder is the AIM-9X, which is more maneuverable and has greater target-seeking abilities than its predecessors.

The Vulcan

For close air-to-air combat, the F-14 has always been equipped with the M61A1 Vulcan Gatling gun, which has been the standard internal aircraft gun of the navy and air force fighter planes for over forty years, starting in 1958 on the F-105 Thunderchief. Its

Technicians load ammunition into the M61A1 Vulcan Gatling gun, which has a range of about a mile. Its rate of fire is up to 6,000 rounds per minute.

20-mm shells pass through six rotating barrels and have a range of approximately one mile (1.6 kilometers). It has a typical rate of fire of 6,000 rounds per minute, although with a drum capacity of only 675 rounds, it would not take very long to run out of bullets!

LANTIRN and Other Guidance Systems

Air-to-air missiles have not been the only combat weapons available to the F-14. In late 1995, the Tomcat took on the new and completely different role as a bomber over targets in Bosnia, thus bringing about a new nickname—the Bombcat. Taking off from the USS *Theodore Roosevelt*, the F-14s dropped laser-guided "smart" bombs (so-called

TARPS ON THE HOME FRONT

The F-14 has used its TARPS capability in at least one nonmilitary mission. In July 1993, two Tomcats were called from their home base of Naval Air Station Oceana in Virginia Beach, Virginia, to monitor the Mississippi River after record rainfall brought the water level up to dangerous levels. The reconnaissance mission's aerial exploration of territory provided photographic evidence of the hardest-hit areas, allowing rescue and relief units to focus their efforts where they were most needed.

for their precision), such as GBU-10/16/24s, each weighing between 1,100 and 2,348 pounds (498.95–1,065 kilograms). The F-14s were accompanied by air force F/A-18s, which illuminated targets for the F-14s with laser designators after dropping their own bomb payloads. When a target is illuminated by a laser beam, the smart bomb will follow that laser straight to the target.

It was the use of the Low Altitude Navigation and Targeting Infrared for Night system (LANTIRN) that enabled the F/A-18s to illuminate the targets. LANTIRN was first delivered to the air force in March 1987 and consists of a navigation pod and a targeting pod. The navigation pod contains a terrain-tracking radar and a fixed infrared sensor, allowing the pilot to receive a clear image of the terrain in front of the aircraft, even at night, and fly along its general contour at high speed, using mountains, valleys, and the cover of darkness to avoid detection. The targeting pod contains a high-resolution infrared sensor, a laser designator range finder for precise delivery of laser-guided weapons, and software for automatic target tracking. The targeting pod can even be used with conventional bombs. Its laser can be pointed at a target to determine the target's location and its distance from the F-14. This information can then be fed into the aircraft's fire control system before the bomb is dropped. The LANTIRN pod system has been widely adopted by the F-14 fleet.

The Tactical Airborne Reconnaissance Pod System (TARPS), an aluminum pod containing sensitive surveillance cameras, can be bolted to F-14s to photograph combat terrain during night and day. It was used during both Operation Desert Storm in the Middle East and Operation Deny Flight in Bosnia-Herzegovina.

TARPS

Sixteen of the F-14s engaged in Operation Desert Storm (see page 29) had been equipped with the Tactical Airborne Reconnaissance Pod System (TARPS). This is an aluminum pod manufactured by the Grumman Corporation containing three infrared camera sensors that are able to film terrain by day or night and in any weather.

Navy F-14s used TARPS in 1993 during Operation Deny Flight in Bosnia-Herzegovina (see page 30), formerly part of the Federal Republic of Yugoslavia. Operating from carriers stationed in the Adriatic Sea, the TARPS-laden F-14s photographed thousands of square miles of disputed territory, which assisted the allied forces in political and military strategy. Aside from TARPS missions, F-14s also flew close air support missions, attacking enemy targets on the ground in Bosnia.

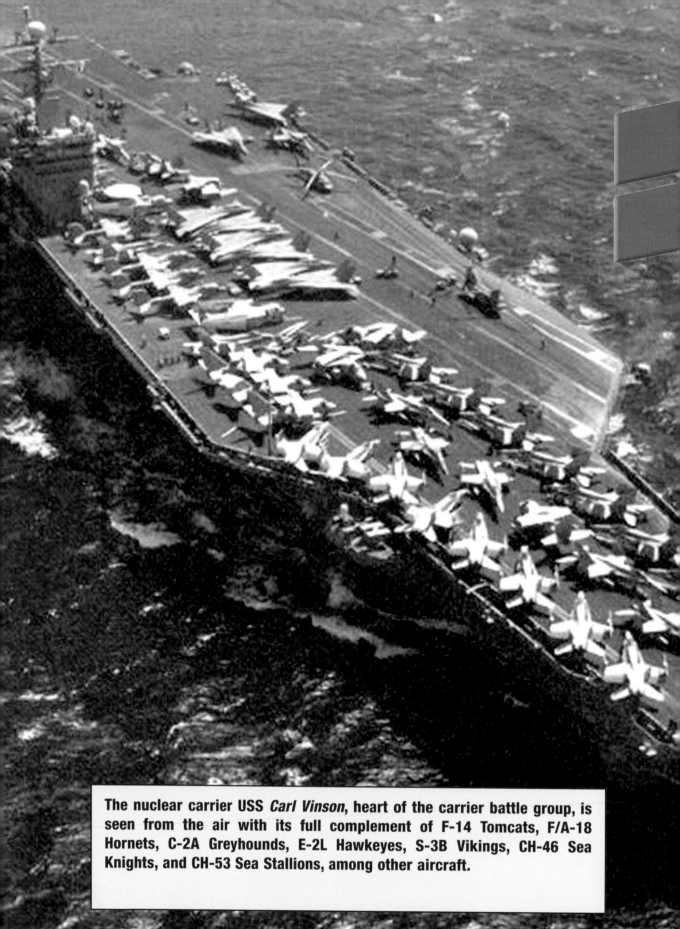

The nuclear carrier USS *Carl Vinson*, heart of the carrier battle group, is seen from the air with its full complement of F-14 Tomcats, F/A-18 Hornets, C-2A Greyhounds, E-2L Hawkeyes, S-3B Vikings, CH-46 Sea Knights, and CH-53 Sea Stallions, among other aircraft.

The word "navy" usually conjures images of battleships plying the waves. The U.S. Navy indeed controls the ships at sea, but it also has a strong presence in the skies. Navy pilots fly various aircraft that are based on certain ships at sea called aircraft carriers, which are like floating runways. Each carrier has a force, called a Carrier Air Wing (or CVW in navy terms), of between seventy-five and ninety-five different aircraft on board at any one time. Each CVW is made up of, for example, fighter aircraft, reconnaissance aircraft, bombers, and helicopters, with the exact composition depending on the particular requirements of the mission under way. Because of the mobility that aircraft carriers provide, navy Tomcats can quickly be deployed to the world's hotspots. As a result, the F-14 has been involved in missions spanning the globe.

The F-14's Combat History

Since the Tomcat first saw action toward the end of the Vietnam War, it has been involved in missions and firefights around the world. After an uneventful start, it quickly proved itself and became the navy's most reliable and versatile fighter plane.

Vietnam

The F-14 was not deployed in Vietnam until late 1974. While it flew combat patrols over South Vietnam, it never shot down any North Vietnamese MiGs (Soviet-made fighter jets).

The Cold War

The primary mission of the F-14 during the Cold War years was to protect the navy's fleet from attack by Soviet bombers. Following formal

The F-14 Tomcat was an invaluable asset to the United States during its conflict with Iraq during the Gulf War. The heavy firepower and speed of the Tomcat deterred any attacks by Iraqi MiG fighters. Tomcats continue to be used in the no-fly zones of northern and southern Iraq to this day.

TOMCAT DOWN

One F-14B, belonging to squadron VF-103 (the "Jolly Rogers"), was shot down by a surface-to-air Iraqi missile. This happened early on the morning of January 21, 1991, forcing the crew, Lieutenants Devon Jones and Larry Slade, to bail out of their Tomcat. An MH-53J helicopter, protected by two air force F-15 Eagle fighters, took off from Arar Airfield in Saudi Arabia and managed to rescue Lieutenant Jones, but Lieutenant Slade was captured by the Iraqis and was not released until March 4, 1991.

rules of engagement, F-14 fighters routinely had to intercept Soviet bombers and fighters that had "accidentally" strayed too close to a carrier battle group and escort them away from the area. This also provided them an opportunity to observe the enemy's planes and weapons from up close.

Libyan Dogfight

In 1981, Libya tried to extend its territorial claim in the Mediterranean Sea to 12 miles (19.2 kilometers) beyond its coast, rather than the internationally accepted 2 miles (3.2 kilometers). The United States challenged this new policy by staging carrier group exercises in the area. U.S. fighters often entered Libyan airspace during these exercises. Libyan fighter planes were occasionally sent up to intercept them. On August 19, 1981, two Libyan Sukhoi Su-22 fighters closed in on a pair of Tomcats. One of the Su-22s fired an air-to-air missile at one of the F-14s, missing it. The Tomcats returned fire. One Libyan plane was hit by a Sidewinder missile. The pilot ejected safely, while the plane crashed to the earth. The second F-14 fired a Sidewinder at the remaining Libyan fighter and destroyed it, killing the pilot.

In 1989, two Libyan MiG-23s were shot down by two Tomcats that were flying close to Libyan airspace. Earlier attempts to warn the Libyan pilots off were unsuccessful, and the American pilots were cleared to fire on them. Both Libyan pilots appeared to eject safely.

An F-14 crew awaits battle, a potential face-off against Libyan MiG-23s during a conflict in 1981. Throughout the 1980s, Libya and the United States did not see eye-to-eye. In 1989, the United States shot down two MiG fighters during a conflict over airspace.

The Gulf War

During the United States-led Gulf War to free Kuwait from Iraqi occupation in 1991, F-14s flew combat air patrols, attacked Iraqi air defenses and SCUD missile launchers, flew reconnaissance missions, and defended the fleet stationed in the Persian Gulf. Iraqi MiGs avoided the F-14s because they were fearful of their powerful radar and Phoenix missiles. As a result, the only F-14 "kill" was the shooting down of an Iraqi MH-53J helicopter.

F-14s continue to patrol the Iraqi no-fly zones in the northern and southern regions of the country. These zones were set up after the war ended in an attempt to ground Iraqi planes and prevent them from attacking Kurdish tribes and other groups living in Iraq that were opposed to President Saddam Hussein's rule.

Armed with two AIM-9 Sidewinders and its LANTIRN targeting system, this F-14 Tomcat comes in for a landing on the deck of the USS *Theodore Roosevelt* in June 1999. The Tomcat was one of many allied planes involved in an assault on Serbian targets during the war in Yugoslavia.

The Balkans

In 1999, as the remnants of the nation formerly known as Yugoslavia continued a bloody ethnic war that involved the massacre of civilians, the North Atlantic Treaty Organization (NATO) decided to get involved. NATO forces would use their airpower to contain the aggressive actions of the Serbs against their neighbors, particularly in Bosnia and Kosovo (where Serbs were accused of engaging in "ethnic cleansing"—taking over land and property belonging to other ethnic groups through forced migration or mass killings). F-14s stationed on carriers in the Adriatic Sea were used to launch air-to-ground attacks on hostile targets, conduct aerial reconnaissance, and—for the first time in their history—deliver precision laser-guided bombs to enemy positions. When the airstrikes came to an end, the F-14s began to provide cover for ground troops.

The War on Terror

Following the September 11, 2001, terrorist attacks on New York City and the Washington, D.C., area U.S. forces, acting in conjunction with a broad-based international coalition, began a series of massive strikes against Afghanistan. This country, ruled by the Taliban, a fundamentalist Islamic group, was accused of harboring and supporting Osama bin Laden and his Al Qaeda terrorists—the group widely believed to be responsible for the September 11 attacks. U.S. aircraft carriers launched long-range, fully loaded F-14s around the clock, sending them deep into Afghanistan where they bombed suspected terrorist bases and training camps, enemy

Massive strikes against Taliban and Al Qaeda forces in Afghanistan were carried out in 2001–2002 by an array of U.S. warplanes, including the F-14 Tomcat.

weapons and vehicles, and Taliban forces. They also provided support for the ground troops of the Northern Alliance—a group of anti-Taliban resistance fighters.

Beginning on September 11, the F-14s also provided a service to Americans that their makers and pilots never envisioned: They patrolled the skies above American cities, keeping a lookout for further waves of hijacked airplanes bent on mass destruction. For more than six months, Tomcats crisscrossed American airspace, policing the skies. In a few cases, they were called upon to escort passenger planes that aroused suspicion for one reason or another. As disorienting as the image of America's mightiest fighter jets

flying over our towns and cities was, they did provide a measure of comfort and security to a rattled nation. The controversial decision to end these flights in March 2002 reminded many Americans of the new sense of national vulnerability. Where once the appearance of Tomcats soaring overhead was disturbing, their sudden disappearance was even more nerve-wracking.

Flight deck crew and pilots prepare for the takeoff of an F-14 from the deck of the USS Enterprise, an aircraft carrier stationed in the Indian Ocean during the U.S. military campaign in Afghanistan between October 2001 and April 2002. F-14s figured heavily during the war effort against the Taliban and Al Qaeda forces.

Pilots who have flown the F-14 have long considered it to be one of the best fighter aircraft currently serving in the U.S. armed forces—or any nation's armed forces, for that matter. It is surprising to learn, then, that the Tomcat is in grave danger of becoming extinct.

Dwindling Interest

In 1988, the navy still seemed squarely behind its fighter. That year it requested that all new F-14 aircraft construction, involving 127 aircraft, follow the specifications of the F-14D model. This meant that all F-14A and A+/B models still using the F-400 engines had to be upgraded to the D model's F110-GE-400 engine.

While these upgrades seemed to indicate that the F-14 still had life in it, economic hard times and pressure to cut costs soon threatened its survival. The revised defense budget submitted to Congress in April 1989 in fact suggested that no new F-14Ds should be built at all, but Congress did authorize eighteen new F-14Ds to be built as long as no more would be requested. As for converting the other models, the schedule accepted by Congress that year allowed for six aircraft to be reconfigured in 1990, twelve in 1991, twenty-four in 1992, forty-eight in 1993, and sixty in 1994, the idea being to have an all-F-14D fleet available by 1998.

Despite studying several other alternatives for low-cost improvement, defense spending cuts scaled back the 1990–1994 F-14A conversion program. The new F-14D construction program was finally terminated in March 1990 by then Secretary of Defense Dick Cheney (later vice president to George W. Bush), only one month after the first F-14D had been delivered to the navy. Almost no new money was made

An F-14 engine is tested on board the USS *Kitty Hawk* on September 12, 2000. In order to remain a potent threat to the armed forces of enemy nations and provide a valuable contribution to national security, the F-14 family of planes has received many upgrades and design improvements over the years.

available for 1991, and none at all was offered in 1992–1993. In mid-February 1991, the navy itself canceled an already funded $780 million contract for 12 remanufactured F-14As, effectively ending the conversion program. The last of the 37 F-14Ds came off the production line on July 20, 1992. Meanwhile, only 18 out of a planned 400 upgraded aircraft were delivered to the navy.

Various plans for advanced versions of the F-14—including the F-14D Quickstrike, the ST21 (Super Tomcat for the 21st Century), the AST21 (Attack Super Tomcat for the 21st Century), and the ASF-14 (Advanced Strike Fighter)—have never gone further than design concepts or scale models. These advanced Tomcats would have offered improved radar systems and infrared navigation and attack sensors, greater range and payload (number of missiles carried), and lighter engines and avionics.

IMPROVING THE TOMCAT

Over the years, various parts and components have been replaced or upgraded on the F-14A. Some of the changes were due to persistent failures or malfunctions; others were simply an attempt to stay on the cutting edge of technology and retain superiority in the skies. As a result, the Tomcat has evolved into a multirole aircraft, encompassing ground attack capability and reconnaissance.

Updated Tomcats received new designations. Here is a list of the various F-14 models and their improvements:

★   F-14A+: Equipped with two General Electric F110-GE-400 engines, a Fatigue Engine Monitoring System, a Threat Warning and Recognition System, and a radar fire control system. These modifications allowed the F-14A+ to take off from a carrier without the use of afterburners, as well as gain greater fuel efficiency, a longer range, and 61 percent greater rate of climb. In 1991, the F-14A+ was redesignated the F-14B.

★   F-14B: Equipped with new Pratt & Whitney F401-P400 engines to replace the trouble-prone TF30 engines. The new engines allowed for acceleration from Mach 0.8 to Mach 1.8 in ninety seconds (making an almost "vertical" acceleration possible) and launch from a carrier deck without the use of afterburners (the flames of which can alert enemies as much as forty miles [sixty-four kilometers] away to a carrier and fighter's presence).

★   F-14C: Equipped with two General Electric F101DFE engines, upgraded avionics, and an improved radar and fire control system. The F-14C was canceled, but these upgrades were later incorporated in the F-14A, F-14A+, and F-14D.

★   F-14D: Equipped with two General Electric F110-GE-400 engines that allow for launch from a carrier without the use of afterburners and provide greater fuel efficiency. Other improvements include an AN/APG-71 radar that has twice the range of the earlier radar and can track up to twenty-four targets simultaneously, a Joint Tactical Information Distribution System (JTIDS) that provides secure communication between the various participants in a mission, an improved heat sensor for detecting and tracking of targets, TARPS pods, and a LANTIRN guidance system.

An Aging Fleet

Fewer than 180 F-14s remain in active service today, out of 712 built for the navy in total. The rest have either crashed or have been retired from service due to aging airframes (which can only be in use for a certain number of flying hours before being put out of service permanently). Originally, each aircraft was designed to fly 6,000 hours, but this has been extended on two occasions to almost 9,000 hours. Once an airframe begins to age, the fighter's operations become more limited. Dogfights, for example, put a lot of g-force stress on the fighter, and cracks may begin to appear, especially where the wings join with the fuselage.

That there have been so many losses and retirements has prompted concern from the public and from Congress about the safety of the aircraft. The navy has countered this criticism by stating that all the available data show that the F-14 is no more prone to serious failure than other fighters. This rather weak defense of the Tomcat may not be enough to save it from the budgetary ax.

On March 2, 2002, the navy once again found itself facing hard questions about the F-14s safety record. On that day, a Tomcat crashed into the Mediterranean Sea just after takeoff from the USS *John F. Kennedy*. The *Kennedy* was on its way to relieve the USS *Theodore Roosevelt* in the Arabian Sea during Operation Enduring Freedom, and was conducting flight training operations fifty miles south of Crete when the crash occurred. Both crew members ejected, but the pilot died after he had been brought back on board the carrier. The radar intercept officer survived.

This latest accident comes after two losses in 2001 and four in 2000, with one of these lost at an air show in Pennsylvania. Almost always, pilot error is identified as the cause of such accidents, with engine failure being the second most common explanation.

The navy expects to retire the older F-14A models by 2004. The more modern F-14B and D models should remain in service until 2010 at least, and possibly until 2015, but the F-14's role as the principal fighter aircraft has already been overtaken by the F/A-18E/F Super Hornet. Designed and built by McDonnell Douglas (now part of Boeing), the Hornet is a single-crew aircraft that, in a single mission, can be competitive in air-to-air combat as well as an effective bomber of targets on the ground, reflecting the military's growing interest in versatile, multiuse aircraft. The Hornet first came into use by the navy, as well as the marines, in 1980.

Yet many navy pilots feel that the F/A-18E/F is too slow and has too short a range. In their opinion, the F-14 is still the most capable

Many critics claim that the F-14 Tomcat has had a less than stellar safety record, pointing to incidents such as the one pictured above. Two crew members and three civilians perished when a navy F-14 crashed into three homes in Nashville, Tennessee, in January 1996. A rescue worker stands in the middle of the wreckage.

fighter aircraft in the categories of attack, intercept, and bombing. They point out that the Tomcat also remains the only fighter that can fulfill both combat and reconnaissance duties.

The fact that the F/A-18E/F Super Hornet has been officially designated as the lead fighter jet of the U.S. armed forces does not mean that the Tomcat has already been consigned to history. Since the end of the Cold War, new threats to regional and global stability and peace have come from developing countries seeking to forcibly gain influence in their own region or aiming to threaten the values held by Western societies.

Since the 1980s, the United States military has been involved in many operations worldwide, from Operation Desert Storm and peace-keeping in the Balkans and Somalia, to Operation Enduring Freedom.

The F/A-18 Hornet has become the plane of choice for many of the United States's most recent military exercises. First deployed in 1980, the Hornet is a single-seat aircraft useful for both dog-fights and bombing expeditions (later models are two-seaters). It remains to be seen whether it will make the F-14, which many still believe has an important role to play, obsolete.

There is no reason to expect that these sorts of conflicts will stop in the coming years. Now that the F-14 has freshly proven its multirole ability to the navy during the war on terrorism in Afghanistan and elsewhere, it may very well remain an important part of any future U.S. military action.

Though its future remains uncertain, there is no doubt that the Tomcat remains one of the most effective, versatile, and technologically sophisticated warplanes ever to take to the skies. It enjoys a stellar track record as an attack and reconnaissance fighter, and has earned a special place in the hearts of Americans for the post–September 11 domestic protection it offered. It is hoped that the Tomcat will long continue to keep America, its soldiers, and its citizens safe from harm, as it has been doing for almost thirty years.

GLOSSARY

afterburner A device attached to a jet's tailpipe that injects fuel into the plane's exhaust gases, providing the jet with extra thrust.

airframe The internal structure of an airplane or missile.

air-to-air missile A missile that is launched from one plane toward another during an attack.

air-to-surface missile A missile launched from an aircraft toward a target on the ground.

avionics The electronics designed for use on an aircraft.

dogfight A fight between two or more fighter planes at close range.

fuselage The central body portion of an aircraft in which the crew, passengers, and cargo are situated.

g-force The force of gravity to which humans are subjected in a vehicle, such as a jet plane, that travels at high speeds.

homing Traveling toward a source of radiated energy, such as heat.

nautical mile An international unit of measure used for sea and air navigation; equal to 6,076.115 feet (1,852 meters).

North Atlantic Treaty Organization (NATO) An alliance of countries (mostly from North America and western Europe) formed in 1949 for the purpose of shared defense and the seeking of peaceful solutions to potential conflicts around the world.

payload The load carried by an aircraft, including passengers, instruments, and weapons.

reconnaissance An exploration of territory for the purpose of gaining information.

surface-to-air missile (SAM) A missile fired from the ground or a ship toward an aircraft or another enemy missile.

FOR MORE INFORMATION

Master Jet Base
Public Affairs Officer
Naval Air Station Oceana
1750 Tomcat Boulevard
Virginia Beach, VA 23460-2191
Web site: http://www.nasoceana.navy.mil

Naval Aviation News
1242 10th Street SE
Washington Navy Yard
Washington, DC 20374-5059
Web site: http://www.history.navy.mil/branches/nhcorg5.htm

Naval Historical Center
Department of the Navy
Washington Navy Yard
805 Kidder Breese Street SE
Washington, DC 20374-5060
Web site: http://www.history.navy.mil

Naval Media Center
2713 Mitscher Road SW
Building 168
Anacostia Annex
Washington, DC 20373-5819
Web site: http://www.mediacen.navy.mil/index.htm

Navy Office of Information
1200 Navy Pentagon
Washington, DC 20350-1200
Web site: http://www.chinfo.navy.mil

Northrop Grumman Corporation
F-14 Administrative Operations
793 Elkridge Landing Road, MS 1660
Linthicum, MD 21090
Web site: http://www.northgrum.com

Smithsonian National Air and Space Museum
7th and Independence Avenue SW
Washington, DC 20560
Web site: http://www.nasm.si.edu

U.S. Air Force Air Combat Command
Public Affairs Office
115 Thompson Street, Suite 211
Langley AFB, VA 23665-1987
Web site: http://www2.acc.af.mil/index.stml

Web Sites

Due to the changing nature of Internet links, the Rosen Publishing Group, Inc., has developed an online list of Web sites related to the subject of this book. This site is updated regularly. Please use this link to access the list:

http://www.rosenlinks.com/usw/tomc/

FOR FURTHER READING

Abramowitz, Melissa. *U.S. Navy at War.* Mankato, MN: Capstone Press, 2001.

Burgan, Michael. *Supercarriers.* Mankato, MN: Capstone Press, 2001.

Gaines, Ann Graham. *The Navy in Action.* New York: Enslow Publishers, 2001.

Green, Michael. *Aircraft Carriers.* Mankato, MN: Capstone Press, 1997.

Green, Michael. *The U.S. Navy.* Mankato, MN: Capstone Press, 1998.

Holden, Henry M. *Navy Combat Aircraft and Pilots.* New York: Enslow Publishers, 2002.

Jefferis, David. *Jets.* Austin, TX: Raintree/Steck-Vaughn, 2001.

Jenssen, Hans, and Moira Butterfield. *Look Inside Cross-Sections: Jets.* New York: DK Publishing, 1996.

Osborn, Shane, and Malcolm McConnell. *Born to Fly: The Heroic Story of Downed U.S. Navy Pilot Lt. Shane Osborn.* New York: Delacorte Books for Young Readers, 2001.

BIBLIOGRAPHY

Anft, Torsten. "The F-14 Tomcat Reference Work." Home of M.A.T.S. 1997–2002. Retrieved March 2002 (http://www.anft.net/f-14/).

Baker, David. *Grumman F-14 Tomcat*. Ramsbury, England: Crowood Press, 1998.

Baugher, Joe. "Grumman F-14 Tomcat." Joe Baugher's Encyclopedia of Military Aircraft. 2001. Retrieved March 2002 (http://www.csd.uwo.ca/~pettypi/elevon/baugher_us/f014.html).

Brown, David F. *Tomcat Alley: A Photographic Roll Call of the Grumman F-14 Tomcat.* Atglen, PA: Schiffer Publishing, Ltd., 1998.

CNN.com. "F-14 Crash Kills U.S. Pilot in Mediterranean." March 2, 2002. Retrieved March 2002 (http://www.cnn.com/2002/US/03/02/tomcat.crash).

Gillcrist, Paul T. *Tomcat! The Grumman F-14 Story.* Atglen, PA: Schiffer Publishing, Ltd., 1994.

Jenkins, Dennis R. *Grumman F-14 Tomcat: Leading U.S. Navy Fleet Fighter.* Leicester, England: Aerofax/Midland Publishing, Ltd., 1997.

Lake, Jon, ed. *Grumman F-14 Tomcat: Shipborne Superfighter.* Westport, CT: Airtime Publishing, 1998.

Reynolds, Clark G. *The Fast Carriers: The Forging of an Air Navy.* Annapolis, MD: United States Naval Institute, 1992.

Rockwell, David L. *Jane's How to Fly the F-14 Tomcat.* New York: HarperCollins, 2001.

INDEX

CREDITS

About the Author

Born in Gloucester, England, Adrian Gardner is interested in writing, traveling, foreign languages and cultures, food, and any combination of the above, especially if his Brooklyn, NYC-born wife, Arthea, can be involved.

Photo Credits

Cover, pp. 4, 10, 13 © David Halford; pp. 5, 6, 9, 16, 19, 30, 39 © AP/Wide World Photos; p. 14 © Nathaniel Miller/U.S. Navy; p. 20 © Jason Scarborough/U.S. Navy; p. 21 © Kimara Scott/U.S. Navy; p. 23 © Photographer's Mate 3rd Class Brian Fleske/U.S. Navy; p. 24 © Carol Warden/U.S. Navy; pp. 26–27 © Corbis; p. 29 © U.S. Navy/ TimePix; p. 31 © Reuters NewMedia, Inc./Corbis; p. 32 © AFP/ Corbis; p. 35 © Chris D. Howell/Corbis; p. 40 © William E. Gortney/U.S. Navy.

Layout and Design

Tom Forget